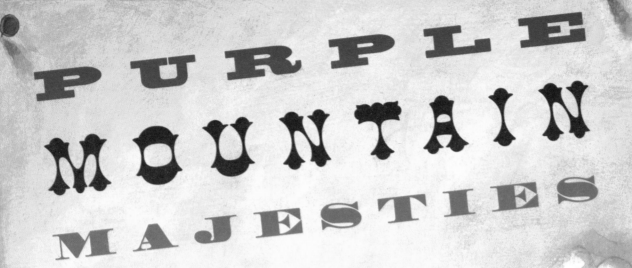

PURPLE MOUNTAIN MAJESTIES

THE STORY OF KATHARINE LEE BATES and "AMERICA THE BEAUTIFUL"

BY BARBARA YOUNGER

ILLUSTRATED BY STACEY SCHUETT

SCHOLASTIC INC.
New York Toronto London Auckland Sydney
Mexico City New Delhi Hong Kong

ISBN 0-439-07665-X

Text copyright © 1998 by Barbara Younger.
Illustrations copyright © 1998 by Stacey Schuett.
All rights reserved.
Published by Scholastic Inc., 555 Broadway, New York, NY 10012,
by arrangement with Dutton Children's Books, a division of Penguin Putnam Inc.
SCHOLASTIC and associated logos are trademarks and/or registered
trademarks of Scholastic Inc.

12 11 10 9 8 7 6 5 4 3 2 1   9/9 0 1 2 3 4/0

Printed in the U.S.A.   08

First Scholastic printing, September 1999

Designed by Amy Berniker

—◆—

ACKNOWLEDGMENTS

With thanks to William Bates, Jr., for his lively letters about his great-aunt Katharine; to Wilma Slaight and Jean Berry, of the Wellesley College Archives, for their help with the Bates Papers; to the schoolchildren who wrote letters to Katharine many years ago, reproduced courtesy of Wellesley College Archives; and to Elizabeth Olmstead, grandniece to Katharine Lee Bates, for granting me permission to quote from her great-aunt's writings.— B.Y.

For my mother and my father,
who took me on a train ride across America when I was a girl,
and for Uncle B, who was waiting when we got there—B.Y.

For Lesly and Clare—S.S.

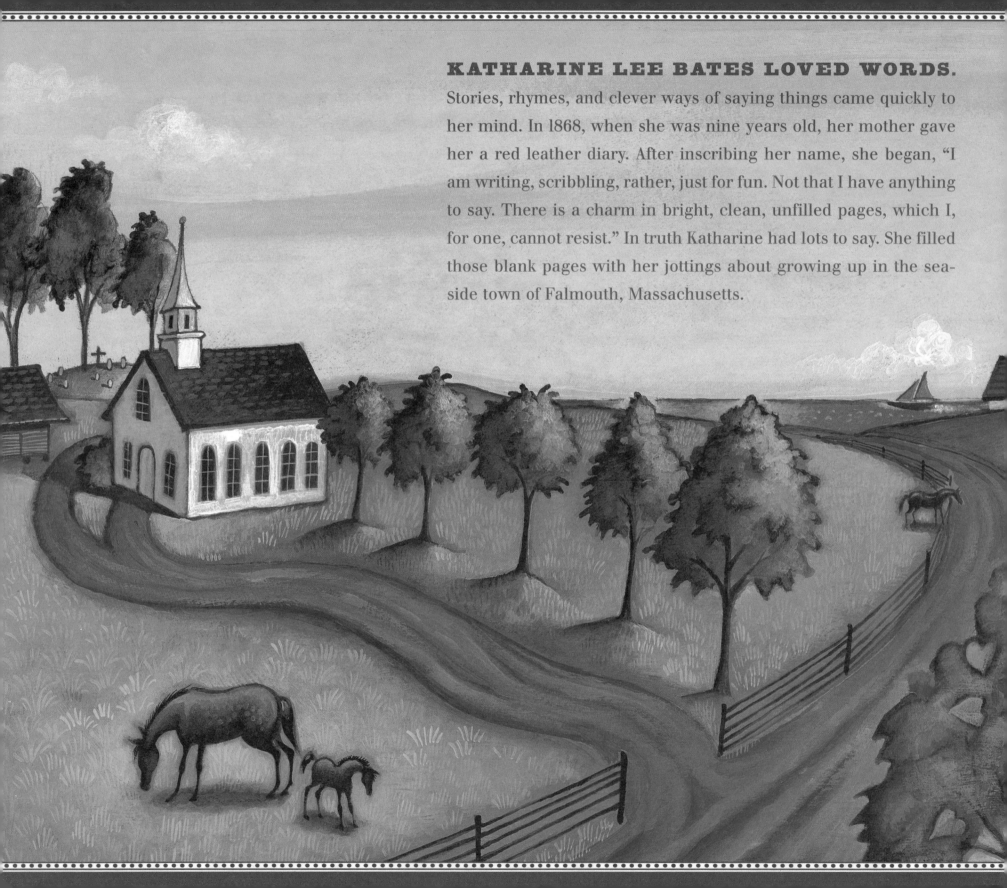

KATHARINE LEE BATES LOVED WORDS.
Stories, rhymes, and clever ways of saying things came quickly to her mind. In 1868, when she was nine years old, her mother gave her a red leather diary. After inscribing her name, she began, "I am writing, scribbling, rather, just for fun. Not that I have anything to say. There is a charm in bright, clean, unfilled pages, which I, for one, cannot resist." In truth Katharine had lots to say. She filled those blank pages with her jottings about growing up in the seaside town of Falmouth, Massachusetts.

KATHARINE'S FATHER HAD DIED WHEN SHE WAS A BABY, AND THE FAMILY
did not have much money. As her older brothers and sister went to work, Katharine, the youngest, helped out at home and kept on writing. In one story of hers, a character mused: "I would study and study. I would know what makes the beautiful colors around you, dear old setting sun, and I would learn all about the nations on the other side of the globe. I would find out why some poetry is poetry and some isn't…and how my head thinks."

Probably Katharine herself felt this way, for she was a witty, imaginative student. With a loan from her brother Arthur, she was able to attend a new college for women called Wellesley. By the time she graduated, she had sold some poems and stories. Later she returned to Wellesley to teach English literature. She wrote poetry all her life. And she did travel—to the British Isles, Europe, Egypt, and the Middle East.

In 1893, when Katharine was thirty-four, she was invited to lecture out west for three weeks in July at a college in Colorado Springs. She accepted eagerly. The extra money would be useful, for by now Katharine was helping to support her mother and sister. And she was glad for the chance to see more of her own country. Of course, she took along her diary and her writing notebooks.

As she settled herself in the train, she must have wondered what adventures the trip would bring. "Left Boston on Fitchburg road at 3 P.M.," she wrote in her diary. She surely did not guess all that lay in store.

THE FOLLOWING DAY THE TRAIN stopped at Niagara Falls. Katharine watched and listened as rivers of water roared and pounded and plunged. On the train that night, she noted, "The glory and music of Niagara Falls." She also wrote a poem about the falls, ending with the lines, *Columnar mist and glistening rainbow play,/A splendid thrill of glory and of peril.*

WHEN THE TRAIN REACHED CHICAGO, KATHARINE was able to spend the weekend with her good friend Katharine Coman, whose family lived in nearby Oak Park. The two women had met at Wellesley, where Miss Coman taught history and economics. Firmly committed to women's education, they were to become close lifelong friends and traveling companions. "We were merry together," Katharine once said.

Katharine respected the social activism of Miss Coman, who came from an Ohio abolitionist family and who wrote, spoke, and organized to improve the conditions of immigrant women laboring in factories and sweatshops. Her friend had a "Westering heart," Katharine wrote, "a vigorous and adventurous personality."

Miss Coman appreciated Katharine's poetry, her devotion to her students, and her vision for a better world. Katharine believed that each person's life held great possibilities. *Dare to dream/Spirit outsoars space,* she urged in one of her poems. Also blessed with a sense of whimsy, Katharine named her bicycle "Lucifer"; often hummed to herself; penned stories and poems for children; read dog books to her own dog; and even hosted a party for parrots on her back steps.

Miss Coman also planned to teach in Colorado Springs that summer. But for now, the two caught up on each other's news and visited friends. Then they went to a fair.

THE FAIR WASN'T JUST ANY FAIR.

It was the World's Columbian Exposition, celebrating the four hundred years that had passed since Christopher Columbus's voyage to the New World. Once the fair was over, the grand-looking buildings, which were made of only thin white plaster, would be taken down. But for now it all gleamed like a magnificent alabaster city. Katharine never forgot it.

THE PURPOSE OF THE FAIR WAS TO SHOW WHAT A GREAT NATION

had grown up in America. Each state had created a display of its own special industries and foods. The California Building featured a knight made entirely of prunes. There were also buildings boasting new machinery, new transportation vehicles, and new inventions such as the zipper. At the Palace of Electricity, many felt the glow of their first electric lamp. In the Anthropological Building, a life-size model of the Great Siberian Mammoth stared down at visitors. The nations of the world set up exhibits, too. The two Katharines admired the dress of people from distant lands.

Impressive though it all was, sadly the fair also reflected the prejudices of the times. African-Americans were provided refreshments and rest rooms only in the Haiti Building. Native Americans appeared in a side show. And no women had been invited to participate in planning the fair. After considerable protest, they were allowed to erect their own building, which they did splendidly with the help of an architect from Boston named Sophia Hayden.

In the distance towered the Wheel, designed by the young engineer George Washington Ferris. Some folks were afraid to ride it, but not the two friends. Time was short, however, so the ride would have to wait until they returned. "The Fair. A thing of beauty. Off again at 6 P.M.," Katharine noted.

THE NEXT DAY, WHICH WAS THE FOURTH OF JULY,
Katharine's New England eyes delighted in the rich amber wheat
fields of the Great Plains rolling by her window. "Hot sirocco run
across Western Kansas," she wrote in her diary, calling herself, "A
better American for such a Fourth." As the train sped west, she
also turned to her notebooks. Her busy schedule had taught her to
write in bits and snatches, her poems often coming "by accident"
in spare moments.

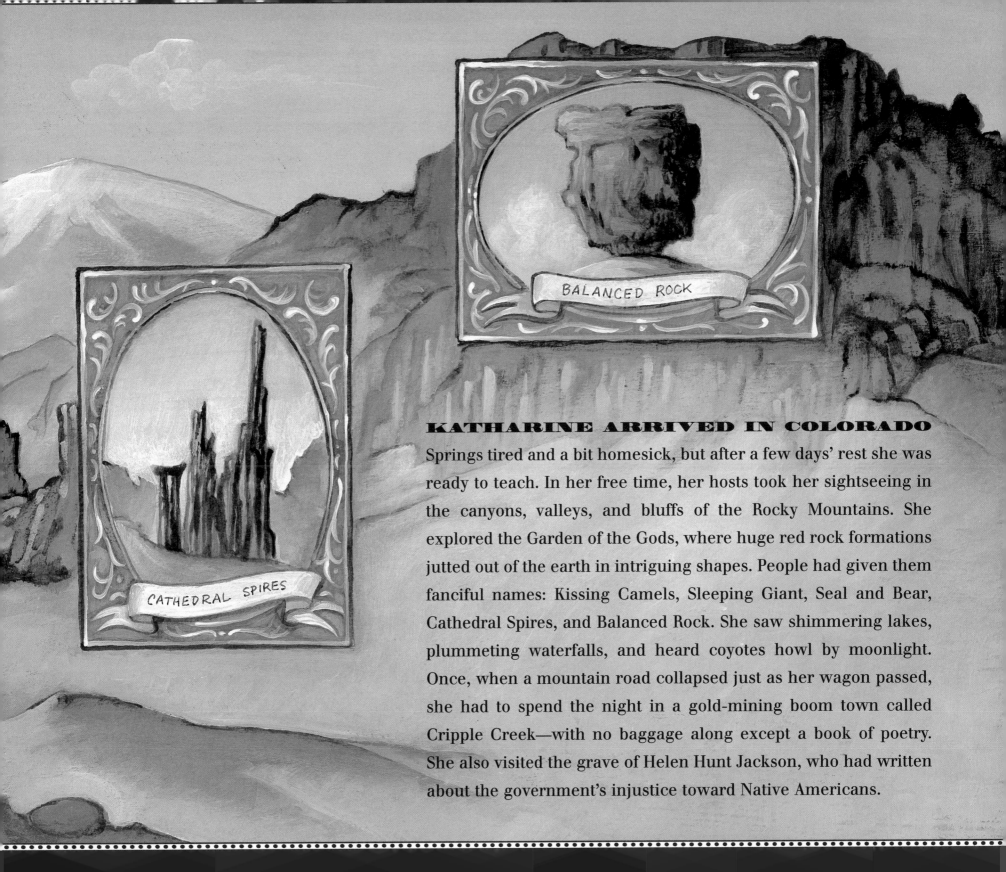

BALANCED ROCK

CATHEDRAL SPIRES

KATHARINE ARRIVED IN COLORADO

Springs tired and a bit homesick, but after a few days' rest she was ready to teach. In her free time, her hosts took her sightseeing in the canyons, valleys, and bluffs of the Rocky Mountains. She explored the Garden of the Gods, where huge red rock formations jutted out of the earth in intriguing shapes. People had given them fanciful names: Kissing Camels, Sleeping Giant, Seal and Bear, Cathedral Spires, and Balanced Rock. She saw shimmering lakes, plummeting waterfalls, and heard coyotes howl by moonlight. Once, when a mountain road collapsed just as her wagon passed, she had to spend the night in a gold-mining boom town called Cripple Creek—with no baggage along except a book of poetry. She also visited the grave of Helen Hunt Jackson, who had written about the government's injustice toward Native Americans.

ONE DAY, KATHARINE AND A GROUP OF
teachers set out for the top of Pikes Peak, a famous mountain that
reached over two and a half miles into the clouds. The rough dirt
road did not go straight up but followed a long and twisty route
with frightening hairpin turns. Now and then a wagon did tip over,
despite the driver's skill. Local people liked to joke that the drivers
didn't need their monthly salaries—relieved tourists, grateful to be
back down safely, made such generous tippers!

The teachers took a train to the base of the mountain. Then the
merry group piled into prairie wagons emblazoned with the slogan
"Pikes Peak or Bust." Halfway up, the drivers stopped at a place
called the Halfway House and exchanged the tired horses for
sturdy mules. The wagons trundled on, up and up, as the pine-
woods gave way to spare "dead white stems, a ghostly forest,"
then rocky land, and finally the summit.

KATHARINE STOOD AND GAZED OUT
at the sea-like expanse of fertile plains below her. She felt the giant arc of the ample skies above. In the distance the Rockies shone purple in the sun. At that moment, the opening lines of a poem floated into her mind.

But no sooner had the words come to her than two teachers began to faint from the altitude. "Quick, into the wagons," the drivers called. So Katharine had only "one brief ecstatic" glimpse from the top of Pikes Peak.

"PIKES PEAK OR BUST," KATHARINE NOTED

in her diary that evening. "Most glorious scenery I ever beheld."
Into her notebook she penciled the lines of poetry that had come
to her that day. *O beautiful for halcyon skies/For amber waves of
grain./ For purple mountain majesties/Above the enameled plain!
America! America! God shed his grace on thee...*

Katharine sat working on more verses. As she wrote, she
remembered her train ride across the country. She thought about
the glory of the land and about the courageous pioneers who had
struggled west in covered wagons to make new lives. She thought
about her own forebears who had crossed the rough Atlantic. She
remembered the Civil War, which had been fought during her
childhood, to end slavery and keep the nation whole. She recalled
the progress and ingenuity exhibited at the fair. But Katharine
knew that beyond that gleaming white city was another city, a
Chicago crowded with hunger and gloom. She had seen that, too.
America was in an economic depression that year. Banks had
closed. Workers were striking. People needed help.

Katharine wrote about a time when "selfish gain" would "no
longer stain" her country. One of her verses went: *O beautiful for
patriot dream/That sees beyond the years/Thine alabaster cities
gleam/Undimmed by human tears!* She knew that it was not always
easy to be fair and loving and to share with others. But her poem
envisioned a country where people would join together out of their
best selves to make life better for everyone.

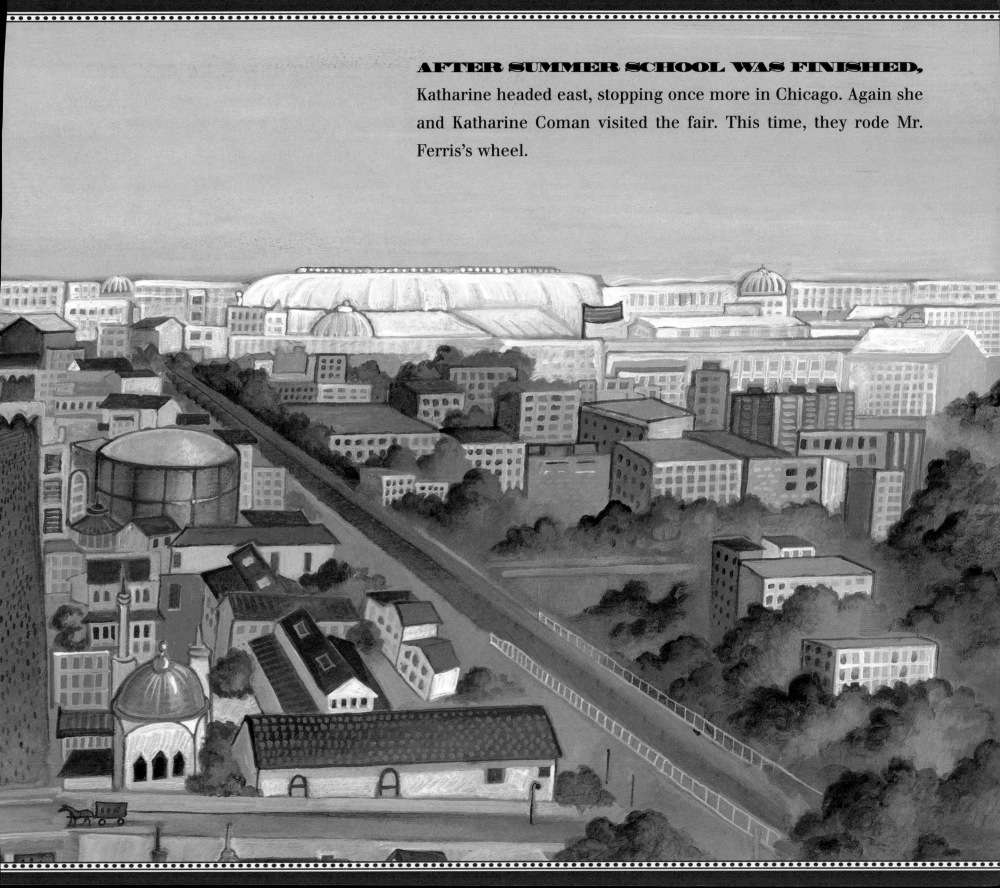

AFTER SUMMER SCHOOL WAS FINISHED,
Katharine headed east, stopping once more in Chicago. Again she and Katharine Coman visited the fair. This time, they rode Mr. Ferris's wheel.

IN EARLY AUGUST KATHARINE ARRIVED BACK IN Wellesley. "Reached home for tea," she jotted. Soon she was busy teaching and laid aside her notebooks from the trip. She wasn't particularly pleased with the poetry she had written that summer. "Consider my verses. Disheartening," she noted in her diary.

Two summers later she came across the Pikes Peak poem and decided to send it to a magazine called *The Congregationalist*. The editor liked it and printed it in the July Fourth issue. Lots of other people liked the poem, too. Almost immediately it was set to many different tunes, even to a march. Soon schools, churches, synagogues, scout troops, and clubs throughout the land were singing Katharine's poem, which was now known as "America the Beautiful." It was even translated so that immigrants new to America could sing it in their own language.

Katharine revised her hymn, as she called it, several times, to make some phrases "more simple and direct" and "a bit more musical." After many years, a contest was held to choose the perfect music, but none of the nine hundred entries seemed just right to the judges. A hymn composed by Samuel Ward is the music we sing today.

AS THE SONG GAINED POPULARITY, PEOPLE
from far and near came to Wellesley to meet Katharine Lee Bates. Over and over she was asked to tell the story of the bumpy ride up the mountain and her moment's glimpse from the top of Pikes Peak. She often invited visitors to stay for tea and to meet her collie dog and parrot. And she showed children treasures from her travels.